Preface

Welcome to the "Oracle Certified Professional Java Programmer OCPJP (Paper Code - 1Z0-809)" guide, a comprehensive resource designed to help you master advanced Java programming and achieve your certification goals. Java remains one of the most sought-after programming languages in the ever-evolving tech industry, and obtaining this certification validates your expertise in Java SE 8. Whether you are an experienced developer refining your skills or a newcomer eager to navigate Java's complexities, this book provides a structured, in-depth exploration of all exam objectives, including lambdas, streams, concurrency, and more.

More than just an exam preparation tool, this book is crafted to deepen your understanding of Java through practical examples, hands-on exercises, and insights from industry experts. Beyond passing the certification, our goal is to equip you with real-world Java development skills that enhance your problem-solving abilities and professional growth. As you embark on this journey, embrace the challenges ahead and let this guide serve as your roadmap to success, positioning you as a certified Java professional ready to excel in the software development landscape.

Table of Contents

OCPJP Practice Questions

1. Which functional interface takes a double value and has a test() method?

a) Double Consumer

b) Double Predicate

c) Double Unary Operator

d) To Double Function

Answer: b

2. The data.doc, data.txt and data.xml files are accessible and contain text. Given the code fragment:

```
Stream<Path> paths = Stream.of (Paths. get("data.doc"),
Paths. get("data.txt"),
Paths. get("data.xml"));
paths.filter(s-> s.toString().endWith("txt")).forEach( s -> {
try { Files.readAllLines(s)
.stream()
.f orEach(System.out::println); //line n1
} catch (IOException e) { System.out.println("Exception");
}
}
);
```

What is the result?

a) The program prints the content of data.txt file.

b) The program prints: Exception<<The content of the data.txt file>> Exception

c) A compilation error occurs at line n1.

d) The program prints the content of the three files.

Answer: a

3. Given:

```
class CheckClass {
```

```
public static int checkValue (String s1, String s2) {
return s1 length() -- s2.length();
}
}
```

and the code fragment:

```
String[] strArray = new String [] {"Tiger", "Rat", "Cat", "Lion"}
//line n1
for (String s : strArray) {
System.out.print (s + " ");
}
```

Which code fragment should be inserted at line n1 to enable the code to print Rat Cat Lion Tiger?

Options

a) Arrays.sort(strArray, CheckClass : : checkValue);

b) Arrays.sort(strArray, (CheckClass : : new) : : checkValue);

c) Arrays.sort(strArray, (CheckClass : : new).checkValue);

d) Arrays.sort(strArray, CheckClass : : new : : checkValue);

Answer :a

4. Given the code fragment:

```
public void recDelete (String dirName) throws
      IOException
      { File [] listOfFiles = new File (dirName)
      . listFiles ( ) ; if (listOfFiles ! = null &&
for (File aFile : listofFiles) {if aFile.isDirectory
recDe1ete (aFi1e .getAbsolutePath else
if (aFi1e.getName ( ) .endsWith ( ". class")) aFi1e.delete
```

Assume that Projects contains subdirectories that contain . class files and is passed as an argument to the recDe1ete() method when it is invoked. What is the result?

a) The method deletes all the . class files in the Proj ects directory

b) and its subdirectories.

c) The method deletes the . class files of the Projects directory only.

d) The method executes and does not make any changes to the Projects directory.

e) The method throws an IOException.

Answer: a

5. Given:

```
public class product { int id; int price;
public Product (int id, int price) { this.id = id;
this.price = price;
}
public String toString() { return id + “:” + price; }
}
```

and the code fragment:

```
List<Product> products = Arrays.asList(new Product(1, 10), new Product (2, 30),
new Product (2, 30));
Product p = products.stream().reduce(new Product (4, 0), (p1, p2) -> { p1.price+=p2.price;
return new Product (p1.id, p1.price);}); products.add(p); products.stream().parallel()
.reduce((p1, p2) - > p1.price > p2.price ? p1 : p2)
.ifPresent(System.out: :println); What is the result?
```

a) 2 : 30

b) 4 : 0

c) 4 : 60

d) 4 : 602 : 303 : 201 : 10

e) The program prints nothing.

Answer: c

6. Given that these files exist and are accessible:

/sports/info.txt

/sports/cricket/players.txt

/sports/cricket/data/ODI.txt

and given the code fragment:

```
int maxDepth =2;
Stream<Path> paths = Files.find(Paths.get("/sports"),
maxDepth,
(p, a) -> p.getFileName().toString().endsWith ("txt"),
FileVisitOption.FOLLOW_LINKS);
Long fCount = paths.count();
System.out.println(fCount);
```

Assuming that there are NO soft-link/symbolic links to any of the files in the directory structure, what is the result?

a) 1

b) 2

c) 3

d) An Exception is thrown at runtime.

Answer: d

7. Given the code fragment:

```
List<String> codes = Arrays.asList ("DOC", "MPEG", "JPEG");
codes.forEach (c -> System.out.print(c + " "));
String fmt = codes.stream()
.filter (s-> s.contains ("PEG"))
.reduce((s, t) -> s + t).get();
System.out.println("\n" + fmt);
```

What is the result?

a) DOC MPEG JPEGMPEGJPEG

b) DOC MPEG MPEGJPEGMPEGMPEGJPEG

c) MPEGJPEGMPEGJPEG

d) The order of the output is unpredictable.

Answer: a

8. Assuming / is the root directory, which of the following are true statements?

a) /home/parrot is an absolute path.

b) /home/parrot is a directory.

c) /home/parrot is a relative path.

d) The path pointed to from a File object must exist.

e) The parent of the path pointed to by a File object must exist.

Answer: a

9. Given the definition of the Vehicle class:

```
Class Vehicle {
	int distance; //line n1
Vehicle (int x) {
this distance = x;
}
public void increSpeed(int time) { //line n2
int timeTravel = time; //line n3
class Car {
int value = 0;
public void speed () {
value = distance /timeTravel;
System.out.println ("Velocity with new speed"+value+"kmph");
}
}
new Car().speed();
}
}
```

and this code fragment:

```
Vehicle v = new Vehicle (100);
v.increSpeed(60);
```

What is the result?

a) Velocity with new speed

b) A compilation error occurs at line n1.

c) A compilation error occurs at line n2.

d) A compilation error occurs at line n3.

Answer : a

10. Given the code fragment:

```
public static void main (String[] args) throws IOException { BufferedReader brCopy = null;
try (BufferedReader br = new BufferedReader (new FileReader("employee.txt")))
{ // line n1
br.lines().forEach(c -> System.out.println(c)); brCopy = br; //line n2
}
brCopy.ready(); //line n3;
}
```

Assume that the ready method of the BufferedReader, when called on a closed BufferedReader, throws an exception, and employee.txt is accessible and contains valid text.

What is the result?

a) A compilation error occurs at line n3.

b) A compilation error occurs at line n1.

c) A compilation error occurs at line n2.

d) The code prints the content of the employee.txt file and throws an exception at line n3.

Answer: d

11. Given that /green.txt and /colors/yellow.txt are accessible, and the code fragment:

```
Path source = Paths.get("/green.txt);
Path target = Paths.get("/colors/yellow.txt);
Files.move(source, target, StandardCopyOption.ATOMIC_MOVE);
Files.delete(source);
```

Which statement is true?

a) The green.txt file content is replaced by the yellow.txt file content and the yellow.txt file is deleted.

b) The yellow.txt file content is replaced by the green.txt file content and an exception is thrown.

c) The file green.txt is moved to the /colors directory.

d) A FileAlreadyExistsException is thrown at runtime.

Answer : d

12. Which two statements are true about the Fork/Join Framework? (Choose two.)

a) The RecursiveTask subclass is used when a task does not need to return a result.

b) The Fork/Join framework can help you take advantage of multicore hardware.

c) The Fork/Join framework implements a work-stealing algorithm.

d) The Fork/Join solution when run on multicore hardware always performs faster than standard sequential solution.

Answer: a, c

13. How do you change the value of an instance variable in an immutable class?

a) Call the setter method.

b) Remove the final modifier and set the instance variable directly.

c) Use a method other than Option Call the setter method. or Remove the final modifier and set the instance variable directly..

d) You can't.

Answer: d

14. Which statement is true about java.time.Duration?

a) It tracks time zones.

b) It preserves daylight saving time.

c) It defines time-based values.

d) It defines date-based values.

Answer: c

15. Given the code fragment:

Path p1 = Paths.get("/Pics/MyPic.jpeg"); System.out.println (p1.getNameCount() + ":" +
p1.getName(1) +
":" + p1.getFileName());

Assume that the Pics directory does NOT exist.

What is the result?

a) An exception is thrown at run time.

b) 2:MyPic.jpeg: MyPic.jpeg

c) 1:Pics:/Pics/ MyPic.jpeg

d) 2:Pics: MyPic.jpeg

Answer: b

16. Given:

IntStream stream = IntStream.of (1,2,3);

IntFunction inFu= x -> y -> x*y; //line n1

IntStream newStream = stream.map(inFu.apply(10)); //line n2

newStream.forEach(System.output::print);

Which modification enables the code fragment to compile?

a) Replace line n1 with:

IntFunction<UnaryOperator> inFu = x -> y -> x*y;

b) Replace line n1 with:

IntFunction<IntUnaryOperator> inFu = x -> y -> x*y;

c) Replace line n1 with:

BiFunction<IntUnaryOperator> inFu = x -> y -> x*y;

a) Replace line n2 with:

IntStream newStream = stream.map(inFu.applyAsInt (10));

Answer:b

17. How do you find out the locale of the running program?

a) Locale.get("default")

b) Locale.get(Locale.DEFAULT)

c) Locale.getDefault()

d) None of the above

Answer: c

18. Given:

```
Book.java:
public class Book {
private String read(String bname) { return "Read" + bname }
}
EBook.java:
public class EBook extends Book {
public class String read (String url) { return "View" + url }
}
Test.java:
public class Test {
public static void main (String[] args) {
Book b1 = new Book();
b1.read("Java Programing");
Book b2 = new EBook();
b2.read("http://ebook.com/ebook");
}
}
```

What is the result?

a) Read Java ProgrammingView http:/ ebook.com/ebook

b) Read Java ProgrammingRead http:/ ebook.com/ebook

c) The EBook.java file fails to compile.

d) The Test.java file fails to compile.

Answer d

19. Which two statements are true about synchronization and locks? (Choose two.)

a) A thread automatically acquires the intrinsic lock on a synchronized statement when executed.

b) The intrinsic lock will be retained by a thread if return from a synchronized method is caused by an uncaught exception.

c) A thread exclusively owns the intrinsic lock of an object between the time it acquires the lock and the time itreleases it.

d) A thread automatically acquires the intrinsic lock on a synchronized method's object when entering that method.

e) Threads cannot acquire intrinsic locks on classes

Answer: a,b

20. Choose the class that is least likely to be marked Serializable.

a) A class that holds data about the amount of rain that has fallen in a given year

b) A class that manages the memory of running processes in an application

c) A class that stores information about apples in an orchard

d) A class that tracks the amount of candy in a gumball machine

Answer: b

21. Which two reasons should you use interfaces instead of abstract classes? (Choose two.)

a) You expect that classes that implement your interfaces have many common methods or fields, or require access modifiers other than public.

b) You expect that unrelated classes would implement your interfaces.

c) You want to share code among several closely related classes.

d) You want to declare non-static on non-final fields.

e) You want to take advantage of multiple inheritance of type.

Answer: b, e

22. When localizing an application, which type of data varies in presentation depending on locale?

a) Dates and Currencies

b) Currencies

c) Dates

d) Neither

Answer: a

23. Given the code fragment:

ZonedDateTime depart = ZonedDateTime.of(2015, 1, 15, 3, 0, 0, 0, ZoneID.of("UTC-7"));

```
ZonedDateTime arrive = ZonedDateTime.of(2015, 1, 15, 9, 0, 0, 0, ZoneID.of("UTC-5"));
long hrs = ChronoUnit.HOURS.between(depart, arrive); //line n1
System.out.println("Travel time is" + hrs + "hours");
```

What is the result?

a) Travel time is 4 hours

b) Travel time is 6 hours

c) Travel time is 8 hours

d) An exception is thrown at line n1.

Answer: a

24. Given the code fragment:

```
List<Integer> values = Arrays.asList (1, 2, 3);
values.stream ()
.map(n -> n*2) //line n1
.peek(System.out::print) //line n2
.count();
```

What is the result?

a) 246

b) The code produces no output.

c) A compilation error occurs at line n1.

d) A compilation error occurs at line n2.

Answer: a

25. Given the definition of the Emp class:

```
public class Emp
private String eName;
private Integer eAge;
Emp(String eN, Integer eA) {
this.eName = eN;
this.eAge = eA;
}
```

```
public Integer getEAge () {return eAge;}
public String getEName () {return eName;}
}
```

and code fragment:

```
List<Emp>li = Arrays.asList(new Emp("Sam", 20), New Emp("John", 60), New Emp("Jim", 51));
Predicate<Emp> agVal = s -> s.getEAge() > 50;//line n1
li = li.stream().filter(agVal).collect(Collectors.toList());
Stream<String> names = li.stream()map.(Emp::getEName);//line n2
names.forEach(n -> System.out.print(n + " "));
```

What is the result?

a) Sam John Jim

b) John Jim

c) A compilation error occurs at line n1.

d) A compilation error occurs at line n2.

Answer: b

26. Given the code fragment:

```
List colors = Arrays.asList("red", "green", "yellow");
Predicate test = n - > {
System.out.println("Searching...");
return n.contains("red");
};
colors.stream()
.filter(c -> c.length() > 3)
.allMatch(test);
```

What is the result?

a) Searching...

b) Searching...Searching...

c) Searching...Searching...Searching...

d) A compilation error occurs.

Answer : a

27. Given: Book.java:

```
public class Book {
private String read(String bname) { return "Read" + bname }
}
EBook.java:
public class EBook extends Book {
public class String read (String url) { return "View" + url }
}
Test.java:
public class Test {
public static void main (String[] args) { Book b1 = new Book();
b1.read("Java Programing"); Book b2 = new EBook();
b2.read("http://ebook.com/ebook");
}
}
```

What is the result?

a) Read Java Programming View http:/ ebook.com/ebook

b) Read Java Programming Read http:/ ebook.com/ebook

c) The EBook.java file fails to compile.

d) The Test.java file fails to compile.

Answer: d

28. Which of the following statements about inheritance and object composition are correct?

a) Inheritance supports access to protected variables.

b) Object composition tends to promote greater code reuse than inheritance.

c) Inheritance relies on the has-a principle.

d) Object composition supports method overriding at runtime.

e) Object composition requires a class variable to be declared public or accessible from a public method to be used by a class in a different package.

f) Object composition is always preferred to inheritance.

Answer: a, b, e

29. Given:

public class Emp { String fName; String lName;

public Emp (String fn, String ln) { fName = fn;

lName = ln;

}

public String getfName() { return fName; } public String getlName() { return lName; }

}

and the code fragment: List<Emp> emp = Arrays.asList (new Emp (“John”, “Smith”),

new Emp (“Peter”, “Sam”),

new Emp (“Thomas”, “Wale”)); emp.stream()

//line n1

.collect(Collectors.toList());

Which code fragment, when inserted at line n1, sorts the employees list in descending order of fName and then ascending order of lName?

a) .sorted (Comparator.comparing(Emp::getfName).reserved().thenComparing(Emp::getlName))

b) .sorted (Comparator.comparing(Emp::getfName).thenComparing(Emp::getlName))

c) .map(Emp::getfName).sorted(Comparator.reserveOrder())

d) .map(Emp::getfName).sorted(Comparator.reserveOrder().map (Emp::getlName).reserved

Answer: a

30. Given:

class UserException extends Exception { }

class AgeOutOfLimitException extends UserException { }

and the code fragment:

class App {

public void doRegister(String name, int age)

throws UserException, AgeOutOfLimitException {

if (name.length () < 6) {

```
throw new UserException ();
} else if (age >= 60) {
throw new AgeOutOfLimitException ();
} else {
System.out.println("User is registered.");
}
}
public static void main(String[ ] args) throws UserException {
App t = new App ();
t.doRegister("Mathew", 60);
}
}
```

What is the result?

a) User is registered.

b) An AgeOutOfLimitException is thrown.

c) A UserException is thrown.

d) A compilation error occurs in the main method.

Answer : b

31. Given the code fragment:

```
public class Foo {
public static void main (String [ ] args) {
Map<Integer, String> unsortMap = new HashMap< > ( );
unsortMap.put (10, "z");
unsortMap.put (5, "b");
unsortMap.put (1, "d");
unsortMap.put (7, "e");
unsortMap.put (50, "j");
Map<Integer, String> treeMap = new TreeMap <Integer, String> (new
Comparator<Integer> ( ) {
@Override public int compare (Integer o1, Integer o2) {return o2.compareTo
```

```
(o1); } } );
treeMap.putAll (unsortMap);
for (Map.Entry<Integer, String> entry : treeMap.entrySet () ) {
System.out.print (entry.getValue () + " ");
}
}
}
```

What is the result?

a) A compilation error occurs.

b) d b e z j

c) j z e b d

d) z b d e j

Answer: c

32. Given the code fragment:

```
public static void main (String [ ] args) throws IOException {
BufferedReader br = new BufferedReader (new InputStremReader (System.in));
System.out.print ("Enter GDP: ");
//line 1
}
```

Which code fragment, when inserted at line 1, enables the code to read the GDP from the user?

a) int GDP = Integer.parseInt (br.readline());

b) int GDP = br.read();

c) int GDP = br.nextInt();

d) int GDP = Integer.parseInt (br.next());

Answer: a

33. What best describes a reduction?

a) A terminal operation where one element is returned from the prior step in a stream pipeline without reading all the elements

b) A terminal operation where a single value is generated by reading each element in the prior step in a stream pipeline

c) An intermediate operation where it mathematically divides each element in the stream

d) An intermediate operation where it filters the stream it receives

Answer: b

34. Given the code fragments:

```
class ThreadRunner implements Runnable {
public void run () { System.out.print ("Runnable") ; }
}
class ThreadCaller implements Callable {
Public String call () throws Exception {return "Callable"; )
}
```

and

```
ExecutorService es = Executors.newCachedThreadPool ();
Runnable r1 = new ThreadRunner ();
Callable c1 = new ThreadCaller ();
// line n1
es.shutdown();
```

Which code fragment can be inserted at line n1 to start r1 and c1 threads?

a) Future<String> f1 = (Future<String>) es.submit (r1);es.execute (c1);

b) es.execute (r1);Future<String> f1 = es.execute (c1) ;

c) Future<String> f1 = (Future<String>) es.execute(r1);Future<String> f2 = (Future<String>) es.execute(c1);

d) es.submit(r1);Future<String> f1 = es.submit (c1);

Answer: d

35. Given the code fragments:

```
class Employee { Optional<Address> address;
Employee (Optional<Address> address) { this.address = address;
}
```

```
public Optional<Address> getAddress() { return address; }
}
class Address {
String city = "New York";
public String getCity { return city: } public String toString() {
return city;
}
}
```

and

```
Address address = null;
Optional<Address> addrs1 = Optional.ofNullable (address);
Employee e1 = new Employee (addrs1);
String eAddress = (addrs1.isPresent()) ? addrs1.get().getCity() : "City Not available";
```

What is the result?

a) New York

b) City Not available

c) null

d) A NoSuchElementException is thrown at run time.

Answer: b

36. Which of the following will print current time?

a) System.out.print(new LocalTime().now());

b) System.out.print(new LocalTime());

c) System.out.print(LocalTime.now());

d) System.out.print(LocalTime.today());

e) None of the above.

Answer: c

37. Given the definition of the Country class:

```
public class country {
public enum Continent {ASIA, EUROPE}String name;
```

```
Continent region;

public Country (String na, Continent reg) { name
= na, region = reg;
}
public String getName () {return name;}public
Continent getRegion () {return region;}
 }
```

and the code fragment:

```
List<Country> couList = Arrays.asList (
new Country ("Japan", Country.Continent.ASIA), new
Country ("Italy", Country.Continent.EUROPE),
new Country ("Germany", Country.Continent.EUROPE));
 Map<Country.Continent, List<String>> regionNames =
 couList.stream ()
       .collect(Collectors.groupingBy (Country
      ::getRegion, Collectors.mapping(Country::getName,
Collectors.toList())));
System.out.println(regionNames);
```

a) {EUROPE = [Italy, Germany], ASIA = [Japan]}

b) {ASIA = [Japan], EUROPE = [Italy, Germany]}

c) {EUROPE = [Germany, Italy], ASIA = [Japan]}

d) {EUROPE = [Germany], EUROPE = [Italy], ASIA = [Japan]}

Answer: b

38. Which two code blocks correctly initialize a Locale variable? (Choose two.)

a) Locale loc1 = "UK";

b) Locale loc2 = Locale.getInstance("ru");

c) Locale loc3 = Locale.getLocaleFactory("RU");

d) Locale loc4 = Locale.UK;

e) Locale loc5 = new Locale ("ru", "RU");

Answer: d, e

39. Given the code fragment:

Path file = Paths.get ("courses.txt");

// line n1

Assume the courses.txt is accessible.

Which code fragment can be inserted at line n1 to enable the code to print the content of the courses.txt file?

a) List<String> fc = Files.list(file); fc.stream().forEach (s - > System.out.println(s));

b) Stream<String> fc = Files.readAllLines (file); fc.forEach (s - > System.out.println(s));

c) List<String> fc = readAllLines(file); fc.stream().forEach (s - > System.out.println(s));

d) Stream<String> fc = Files.lines (file); fc.forEach (s - > System.out.println(s));

Answer: d

40. What is a common reason for a stream pipeline not to run?

a) The source doesn't generate any items.

b) There are no intermediate operations.

c) The terminal operation is missing.

d) None of the above

Answer: c

41. Given:

class Book { int id;

String name;

public Book (int id, String name) { this.id = id;

this.name = name;

}

public boolean equals (Object obj) { //line n1 boolean output = false;

Book b = (Book) obj;

if (this.name.equals(b name))} output = true;

}

return output;

}

}

and the code fragment:

Book b1 = new Book (101, “Java Programing”); Book b2 = new Book (102, “Java Programing”); System.out.println (b1.equals(b2)); //line n2 Which statement is true?

a) The program prints true.

b) The program prints false.

c) A compilation error occur

d) To ensure successful compilation, replace line n1 with:boolean equals (Book obj) {

e) A compilation error occur

f) To ensure successful compilation, replace line n2 with: System.out.println (b1.equals((Object) b2));

Answer: a

42. Given the code fragment:

List<String> listVal = Arrays.asList(“Joe”, “Paul”, “Alice”, “Tom”); System.out.println (

// line n1

);

Which code fragment, when inserted at line n1, enables the code to print the count of string elements whose length is greater than three?

a) listVal.stream().filter(x -> x.length()>3).count()

b) listVal.stream().map(x -> x.length()>3).count()

c) listVal.stream().peek(x -> x.length()>3).count().get()

d) listVal.stream().filter(x -> x.length()>3).mapToInt(x -> x).count()

Answer: a

43. Given the code fragment:

public static void main (String[] args) {

Stream. of ("Java” , "Unix", " Linux ")

. fliter (s —> s. contains ("n"))

.peek(s—> System. out . println ("PEEK: " +s))

// line n 1

}

Which two code fragments, when inserted at line n1 independently, result in the output PEEK: Unix?

a) .anyMatch ();

b) .allMatch ();

c) .findAny ();

d) .noneMatch ();

e) .findFirst ();

Answer: e

44. Given:

public class Customer { private String fName; private String lName; private static int count;

public customer (String first, String last) {fName = first, lName = last;

++count;}

static { count = 0; }

public static int getCount() {return count; }

}

public class App {

public static void main (String [] args) { Customer c1 = new Customer("Larry", "Smith");

Customer c2 = new Customer("Pedro", "Gonzales"); Customer c3 = new Customer("Penny", "Jones"); Customer c4 = new Customer("Lars", "Svenson"); c4 =

null;

c3 = c2;

System.out.println (Customer.getCount());

}

}

What is the result?

a) 2

b) 3

c) 4

d) 5

Answer: d

45. What is true about the java.sql.Statement interface?

a) It provides a session with the database.

b) It is used to get an instance of a Connection object by using JDBC drivers.

c) It provides a cursor to fetch the resulting data.

d) It provides a class for executing SQL statements and returning the results.

Answer: d

46. Given the definition of the Book class

```
public class Book {
    private int id;
    private string name;
    public Book (int id, String name) {this. id= id; this. name= name; }
    public int getId() { return id; }
    public String getName ( ) { return name; }
    public void set Id (int id) { this. id = id; }
    public void setName (String name) { this . name= name;}
    }
```

Which statement is true about the Book class?

a) It demonstrates encapsulation.

b) It is defined using the factory design pattern.

c) It is defined using the singleton design pattern.

d) It demonstrates polymorphism.

e) It is an immutable class.

Answer: a

47. Given the content of /resourses/Message.properties: welcome1="Good day!"
and given the code fragment: Properties prop = new Properties ();
FileInputStream fis = new FileInputStream ("/resources/Message.properties"); prop.load(fis);
System.out.println(prop.getProperty("welcome1"));
System.out.println(prop.getProperty("welcome2", "Test"));//line n1
System.out.println(prop.getProperty("welcome3"));
What is the result?

a) Good day!Testfollowed by an Exception stack trace

b) Good day!followed by an Exception stack trace

c) Good day!Test null

d) A compilation error occurs at line n1.

Answer: c

48. Given the code fragment: public class Foo {
public static void main (String [ ] args) {
Map<Integer, String> unsortMap = new HashMap< > ( ); unsortMap.put (10, "z");
unsortMap.put (5, "b");
unsortMap.put (1, "d");
unsortMap.put (7, "e");
unsortMap.put (50, "j");
Map<Integer, String> treeMap = new TreeMap <Integer, String> (new Comparator<Integer> ( )
{
@Override public int compare (Integer o1, Integer o2) {return o2.compareTo
(o1); } });
treeMap.putAll (unsortMap);
for (Map.Entry<Integer, String> entry : treeMap.entrySet ()) { System.out.print (entry.getValue
() + " ");
}
}
}

What is the result?

a) A compilation error occurs.

b) d b e z j

c) j z e b d

d) z b d e j

Answer: c

49. Given the definition of the Emp class: public class Emp

private String eName; private Integer eAge;

Emp(String eN, Integer eA) { this.eName = eN;

this.eAge = eA;

}

public Integer getEAge () {return eAge;} public String getEName () {return eName;}

}

and code fragment:

List<Emp>li = Arrays.asList(new Emp("Sam", 20), New Emp("John", 60), New Emp ("Jim", 51));

Predicate<Emp> agVal = s -> s.getEAge() > 50; //line n1 li =

li.stream().filter(agVal).collect(Collectors.toList());

Stream<String> names = li.stream()map.(Emp::getEName); //line n2 names.forEach(n ->

System.out.print(n + " "));

What is the result?

a) Sam John Jim

b) John Jim

c) compilation error occurs at line n1.

d) A compilation error occurs at line n2.

Answer: b

50. Given:

public class Canvas implements Drawable { public void draw () { }

}

```
public abstract class Board extends Canvas { }
public class Paper extends Canvas { protected void draw (int color) { }
}
public class Frame extends Canvas implements Drawable { public void resize () { }
}
public interface Drawable { public abstract void draw ();
}
```

Which statement is true?

a) Board does not compile.

b) Paper does not compile.

c) Frame does not compile.

d) Drawable does not compile.

e) All classes compile successfully.

Answer: e

51. Given the code fragments:

```
class MyThread implements Runnable {
private static AtomicInteger count = new AtomicInteger (0); public void run () {
int x = count.incrementAndGet(); System.out.print (x+" ");
}
}
```

and

```
Thread thread1 = new Thread(new MyThread()); Thread thread2 = new Thread(new
MyThread()); Thread thread3 = new Thread(new MyThread()); Thread [] ta =
{thread1, thread2, thread3};
for (int x= 0; x < 3; x++) { ta[x].start();
}
```

Which statement is true?

a) The program prints 1 2 3 and the order is unpredictable.

b) he program prints 1 2 3.

c) The program prints 1 1 1.

d) A compilation error occurs.

Answer: a

52. You want to create a singleton class by using the Singleton design pattern. Which two statements enforce the singleton nature of the design? (Choose two.)

a) Make the class static.

b) Make the constructor private.

c) Override equals() and hashCode() methods of the java.lang.Object class.

d) Use a static reference to point to the single instance.

e) Implement the Serializable interface.

Answer: b, d

53. You have been asked to create a ResourceBundle which uses a properties file to localize an application. Which code example specifies valid keys of menu1 and menu2 with values of File Menu and View Menu?

a) <key name = ‘menu1”>File Menu</key><key name = ‘menu2”>View Menu</key>

b) <key>menu1</key><value>File Menu</value><key>menu2</key><value>View Menu</value>

c) menu1, File Menu, menu2, View Menu Menu

d) menu1 = File Menu menu2 = View Menu

Answer: d

54. Locale Currency Symbol Currency Code

US $ USD

and the code fragment?

double d = 15;

Locale l = new Locale (“en”, “US”);

NumberFormat formatter = NumberFormat. getCurrencyInstance(l) ;

System.out.println(formatter.format(d));

What is the result?

a) $15.00

b) 15 $

c) USD 15.00

d) USD $15

Answer: a

55. Given the content of /resourses/Message.properties: welcome1="Good day!"

and given the code fragment: Properties prop = new Properties ();

FileInputStream fis = new FileInputStream ("/resources/Message.properties"); prop.load(fis);

System.out.println(prop.getProperty("welcome1"));

System.out.println(prop.getProperty("welcome2", "Test"));//line n1

System.out.println(prop.getProperty("welcome3"));

What is the result?

a) Good day!Testfollowed by an Exception stack trace

b) Good day!followed by an Exception stack trace

c) Good day!Test null

d) A compilation error occurs at line n1.

Answer: c

56. Given the structure of the STUDENT table: Student (id INTEGER, name VARCHAR)

Given:

public class Test {

static Connection newConnection =null;

public static Connection get DBConnection () throws SQLException { try (Connection con = DriveManager.getConnection(URL, username, password)) {

newConnection = con;

}

return newConnection;

}

public static void main (String [] args) throws SQLException { get DBConnection ();

Statement st = newConnection.createStatement(); st.executeUpdate("INSERT INTO student VALUES (102, 'Kelvin')");

}

}

Assume that:

The required database driver is configured in the classpath.

The appropriate database is accessible with the URL, userName, and passWord exists. The SQL query is valid.

What is the result?

a) The program executes successfully and the STUDENT table is updated with one record.

b) The program executes successfully and the STUDENT table is NOT updated with any record.

c) A SQLException is thrown as runtime.

d) A NullPointerException is thrown as runtime.

Answer: c

57. Which statement is true about the DriverManager class?

a) It returns an instance of Connection.

b) it executes SQL statements against the database.

c) It only queries metadata of the database.

d) it is written by different vendors for their specific database.

Answer: a

58. Which code fragment is required to load a JDBC 3.0 driver?

a) Connection con = Connection.getDriver ("jdbc:xyzdata://localhost:3306/EmployeeDB");

b) Class.forName("org.xyzdata.jdbc.NetworkDriver");

c) Connection con = DriverManager.getConnection ("jdbc:xyzdata://localhost:3306/EmployeeDB");

d) DriverManager.loadDriver ("org.xyzdata.jdbc.NetworkDriver");

Answer: b

59. Given the code fragments:

interface CourseFilter extends Predicate<String> { public default boolean test (String str) {

return str.equals ("Java");

}

}

and

List<String> strs = Arrays.asList("Java", "Java EE", "Java ME"); Predicate<String> cf1 = s - >

s.length() > 3;

Predicate cf2 = new CourseFilter() { //line n1 public boolean test (String s) {

return s.contains ("Java");

}

};

long c = strs.stream()

.filter(cf1)

.f ilter(cf2 //line n2

.count(); System.out.println(c); What is the result?

a) 2

b) 3

c) A compilation error occurs at line n1.

d) A compilation error occurs at line n2.

Answer: b

60. Given:

```
public class Vehicle {
    int vld;
    String vName;
    public Vehicle (int vldArg, String vNameArg) {
```

```
this.vId = vldArg;
this.vName= vNameArg ;
      }
      public int getVId() { return vld; }
      public String getVName ( ) { return vName ;}
      public String toString() {
      return vName;
 }
}
```

and the code fragment:

```
List<Vehicle> vehicle = Arrays.asList(
                new Vehicle (2,  "Car"),
          new Vehicle (3, "Bike"),
          new Vehicle (1, "Truck") );
vehicle.stream()
          //linen1
          .forEach(System.out::print);
```

Which two code fragments, when inserted at line n1 independently, enable the code to print TruckCarBike?

a) .sorted ((v1, v2) -> v1.getVId() < v2.getVId())

b) .sorted (Comparable.comparing (Vehicle: :getVName)).reversed ()

c) .map (v -> v.getVid()).sorted ()

d) .sorted((v1, v2) -> Integer.compare(v1.getVId(), v2.getVid()))

e) .sorted(Comparator.comparing ((Vehicle v) -> v.getVId()))

Answer: b

61. Given the code fragment

```
//line n1
System.out.println(iP);
```

Which code fragment, when inserted at line n1, enables the code to print /First.txt?

a) Path iP = new Paths (“/First.txt”);

b) Path iP = Paths.toPath (“/First.txt”);

c) Path iP = new Path (“/First.txt”);

d) Path iP = Paths.get (“/”, “First.txt”);

Answer: d

62. Given the code fragments: class Employee { Optional<Address> address;

Employee (Optional<Address> address) { this.address = address;

}

public Optional<Address> getAddress() { return address; }

}

class Address {

String city = “New York”;

public String getCity { return city: } public String toString() {

return city;

}

}

and

Address address = null;

Optional<Address> addrs1 = Optional.ofNullable (address);

Employee e1 = new Employee (addrs1);

String eAddress = (addrs1.isPresent()) ? addrs1.get().getCity() : “City Not available”;

What is the result?

a) New York

b) City Not available

c) null

d) A NoSuchElementException is thrown at run time.

Answer: b

63. Given:

class CheckClass {

public static int checkValue (String s1, String s2) { return s1 length() – s2.length();

}

}

and the code fragment:

String[] strArray = new String [] {“Tiger”, “Rat”, “Cat”, “Lion”}

//line n1

for (String s : strArray) { System.out.print (s + “ “);

}

Which code fragment should be inserted at line n1 to enable the code to print Rat Cat Lion Tiger?

a) Arrays.sort(strArray, CheckClass : : checkValue);

b) Arrays.sort(strArray, (CheckClass : : new) : : checkValue);

c) Arrays.sort(strArray, (CheckClass : : new).checkValue);

d) Arrays.sort(strArray, CheckClass : : new : : checkValue);

Answer: a

64. Given:

interface P {public void method1(); }

interface Q extends P {public void method2 (); }

interface R extends P {public void method2 (); }

interface S {public default void method () { } }

interface T {public void method1 (); public void method2 (); }

interface U {public void method1 (); public abstract void method2 ();

Which two interfaces can you use to create lambda expressions? (Choose two.)

a) T

b) R

c) P

d) S

e) Q

f) U

Answer: a, f

65. In 2015, daylight saving time in New York, USA, begins on March 8th at 2:00 AM. As a result, 2:00 AM becomes 3:00 AM.

Given the code fragment:

```
ZoneId zone = ZoneId .of( America/ New_York");
ZonedDateTime dt = ZonedDateTime.of (LocalDate.of (2015,3, 8), LocalTime.of (1, 0),
zone);
ZonedDateTime dt2 = dt.p1usHours (2) ;
System. out. print (DateTimeFormatter. ofPattern ( "H:mm – "). format (dt2) ) ;
System.out.println ("difference: " + ChronoUnit.HOURS.between (dt, dt2) ) ;
```

Which is the result?

a) 3:00 – difference: 2

b) 2:00 – difference: 1

c) 4:00 – difference: 3

d) 4:00 – difference: 2

Answer: b

66. Given:

```
interface Interface1 {
                public default void sayHi ( ) {
System. out ("Hi Interface- 1") ;
                }
        }
public class MyClass implements Interface1, Interf ace2
    public static void main (String []  args) {
        Interface1 obj = new MyClass ( ) ;
         obj . sayHi ( ) ;
      }
  public void sayHi() {
        System. out. println ("Hi MyC1ass") ;
```

```
}
}
```

What is the result?

a) Hi Interface-2

b) A compilation error occurs.

c) Hi Interface-1

d) Hi MyClass

Answer: d

67. Given the code fragment:

```
Path source = Paths.get (“/data/december/log.txt”); Path destination = Paths.get(“/data”);
Files.copy (source, destination);
```

and assuming that the file /data/december/log.txt is accessible and contains: 10-Dec-2014 – Executed successfully

What is the result?

a) A file with the name log.txt is created in the /data directory and the content of the /data/december/ log.txt file is copied to it.

b) The program executes successfully and does NOT change the file system.

c) A FileNotFoundException is thrown at run time.

d) A FileAlreadyExistsException is thrown at run time.

Answer: d

68. Given the code fragment:

```
Stream<List<String>> strs = Stream.of (
        Arrays. asList(“text1”, “text2”),
        Arrays. asList(“text2”, “text3”));
Stream<String>bs2= strs
        .filter(b -> b.contains(“text1”) )
        .flatMap(rs -> rs.stream());
bs2. forEach(b -> System.out.print(b)) ;
```

What is the result?

a) text1text2

b) text1text2text2text3

c) text1

d) [text1, text2]

Answer: a

69. Given the code fragment: Stream<List<String>> iStr= Stream.of (Arrays.asList ("1", "John"),

Arrays.asList ("2", null)0;

Stream<<String> nInSt = iStr.flatMapToInt ((x) -> x.stream ()); nInSt.forEach (System.out :: print);

What is the result?

a) 1John2null

b) 12

c) A NullPointerException is thrown at run time.

d) A compilation error occurs.

Answer: d

70. Given:

class Student {

String course, name, city;

public Student (String name, String course, String city) { this.course = course; this.name = name; this.city = city;

}

public String toString() {

return course + ":" + name + ":" + city;

}

and the code fragment:

List<Student> stds = Arrays.asList(

new Student (“Jessy”, “Java ME”, “Chicago”), new Student (“Helen”, “Java EE”, “Houston”),

new Student (“Mark”, “Java ME”, “Chicago”)); stds.stream()

.collect(Collectors.groupingBy(Student::getCourse))

.f orEach(src, res) -> System.out.println(scr));

What is the result?

a) [Java EE: Helen:Houston][Java ME: Jessy:Chicago, Java ME: Mark:Chicago]

b) Java EEJava ME

c) [Java ME: Jessy:Chicago, Java ME: Mark:Chicago] [Java EE: Helen:Houston]

d) A compilation error occurs.

Answer: b

71. Given the code fragment:

List<String> colors = Arrays.asList(“red”, “green”, “yellow”); Predicate<String> test = n - > {

System.out.println(“Searching…”);

return n.contains(“red”);

};

colors.stream()

.f ilter(c -> c.length() > 3)

.allMatch(test);

What is the result?

a) Searching...

b) Searching...Searching...

c) Searching...Searching... Searching...

d) A compilation error occurs.

Answer: a

72. Given:

public enum USCurrency { PENNY (1),

NICKLE(5), DIME (10), QUARTER(25);

private int value;

public USCurrency(int value) { this.value = value;

```
}
public int getValue() {return value;}
}
public class Coin {
public static void main (String[] args) { USCurrency usCoin =new USCurrency.DIME;
System.out.println(usCoin.getValue()):
}
}
```

Which two modifications enable the given code to compile? (Choose two.)

a) Nest the USCurrency enumeration declaration within the Coin class.

b) Make the USCurrency enumeration constructor private.

c) Remove the new keyword from the instantion of usCoin.

d) Make the getter method of value as a static method.

e) Add the final keyword in the declaration of value.

Answer: b, c

73. Given the definition of the Country class: public class country {

```
public enum Continent {ASIA, EUROPE} String name;
Continent region;
public Country (String na, Continent reg) { name = na, region = reg;
}
public String getName () {return name;} public Continent getRegion () {return region;}
}
```

and the code fragment:

```
List<Country> couList = Arrays.asList (
new Country ("Japan", Country.Continent.ASIA), new Country ("Italy",
Country.Continent.EUROPE),
new Country ("Germany", Country.Continent.EUROPE)); Map<Country.Continent,
List<String>> regionNames = couList.stream () collect(Collectors.groupingBy (Country
::getRegion, Collectors.mapping(Country::getName, Collectors.toList())));
System.out.println(regionNames);
```

a) {EUROPE = [Italy, Germany], ASIA = [Japan]}

b) {ASIA = [Japan], EUROPE = [Italy, Germany]}

c) {EUROPE = [Germany, Italy], ASIA = [Japan]}

d) {EUROPE = [Germany], EUROPE = [Italy], ASIA = [Japan]}

Answer: b

74. Given that these files exist and are accessible:

/company/emp/info.txt

/company/emp/benefits/b1.txt

and given the code fragment:

// line n1

Stream.forEach(s ->System.out.print (s));

Which code fragment can be inserted at line n1 to enable the code to print only /company/emp?

a) Stream<Path> stream = Files.list (Paths.get ("/company"));

b) Stream<Path> stream = Files.find(Paths.get ("/company"), 1,(p,b) –> b.isDirectory (), FileVisitOption.FOLLOW_LINKS);

c) Stream<Path> stream = Files.walk (Paths.get ("/company"));

d) Stream<Path> stream = Files.list (Paths.get ("/company/emp"));

Answer: b

75. Given the code fragment:

List<String> nL = Arrays.asList("Jim", "John", "Jeff"); Function<String, String> funVal = s -> "Hello : ".contact(s); nL.Stream()

.map(funVal)

.peek(System.out::print); What is the result?

a) Hello : Jim Hello : John Hello : Jeff

b) Jim John Jeff

c) The program prints nothing.

d) A compilation error occurs.

Answer: c

76. Given:

```
class RateOfInterest {
public static void main (String[] args) { int rateOfInterest = 0;
String accountType = "LOAN"; switch (accountType) {
case "RD"; rateOfInterest = 5; break;
case "FD"; rateOfInterest = 10; break;
default:
assert false: "No interest for this account"; //line n1
}
System.out.println ("Rate of interest:" + rateOfInterest);
}
}
```

and the command:

java –ea RateOfInterest

What is the result?

a) Rate of interest: 0

b) An AssertionError is thrown.

c) No interest for this account

d) A compilation error occurs at line n1.

Answer: b

77. Given:

Item table

- ID, INTEGER: PK
- DESCRIP, VARCHAR(100)
- PRICE, REAL
- QUANTITY< INTEGER

And given the code fragment:

```
try {
```

```
Connection conn = DriveManager.getConnection(dbURL, username, password);
String query = "Select * FROM Item WHERE ID = 110";
Statement stmt = conn.createStatement();
ResultSet rs = stmt.executeQuery(query);
while(rs.next()) {
System.out.println("ID: " + rs.getInt("Id"));
System.out.println("Description: " + rs.getString("Descrip"));
System.out.println("Price: " + rs.getDouble("Price"));
System.out.println(Quantity: " + rs.getInt("Quantity"));
}
} catch (SQLException se) {
System.out.println("Error");
}
```

Assume that:

The required database driver is configured in the classpath.

The appropriate database is accessible with the dbURL, userName, and passWord exists. The SQL query is valid.

What is the result?

a) An exception is thrown at runtime.

b) Compilation fails.

c) The code prints Error.

d) The code prints information about Item 110.

Answer: d

78. Given the code fragment:

```
Deque<String> queue = new ArrayDeque<> () ;
queue. add (" Susan ");
queue. add (" Allen ");
queue. add (" David ");
System.out. println(queue.pop());
System.out. println(queue.remove());
```

```
System.out. println(queue);
```

What is the result?

a) DavidDavid[Susan, Allen]

b) SusanSusan[Susan, Allen]

c) SusanAllen [David]

d) DavidAllen [Susan]

e) SusanAllen[Susan, David]

Answer: c

79. Given the code fragment:

```
// Login time:2015-01-12T21:58:18.817z
Instant loginTime =  Instant .now ( ) ;
Thread. sleep (1000);

// Logout time:2015-01-12T21: 58:19.880z
Instant logoutTime = Instant.now();

loginTime = logTime.truncatedTo(ChronoUnit.Minutes);    //line n1
        logoutTime = logoutTime.truncatedTo(ChronoUnit.Minutes);

if (logoutTime isAfter (loginTime) )
   System. out. println ("Logged out at: "+logoutTime) ;
else
   System. out . println("Can't logout") ;
```

What is the result?

a) A compilation error occurs at line n1.

b) Logged out at: 2015-01-12T21:58:19.880Z

c) Can't logout

d) Logged out at: 2015-01-12T21:58:00Z

Answer: d

80. Given the code fragments: class TechName {

String techName;

TechName (String techName) { this.techName=techName; }

}

and

List<TechName> tech = Arrays.asList (new TechName(“Java-“),

new TechName(“Oracle DB-“), new TechName(“J2EE-“)

);

Stream<TechName> stre = tech.stream();

//line n1

Which should be inserted at line n1 to print Java-Oracle DB-J2EE-?

a) stre.forEach(System.out::print);

b) stre.map(a-> a.techName).forEach(System.out::print);

c) tre.map(a-> a).forEachOrdered(System.out::print);

d) stre.forEachOrdered(System.out::print);

Answer: b

81. Given the code fragment:

Map<Integer, Integer> mVal = new HashMap<> ();

mVal.put(1, 10);

mVal.put(2, 20);

//line n1

c.accept (1, 2);

mVal.forEach(c);

Which statement can be inserted into line n1 to print 1,2; 1,10; 2,20;?

a) BiConsumer<Integer,Integer> c = (i, j) -> {System.out.print (i + “,” + j+ “; “);};

b) BiFunction<Integer, Integer, String> c = (i, j) –> {System.out.print (i + “,” + j+ “; “)};

c) BiConsumer<Integer, Integer, String> c = (i, j) –> {System.out.print (i + “,” + j+ “; “)};

d) BiConsumer<Integer, Integer, Integer> c = (i, j) –> {System.out.print (i + “,”+ j+ “; “);};

Answer: b

82. Given

```
public class StrMan {
        public static void doStuff(String s) {
                try {
                        if (s= = null) {
throw new NullPointerException();
}
                                } finally {
                                  System.out.println("-finally-");
                                }
                          System.out.println("-doStuff-");
        }
                public static void main (Sting[] args) {
                        try{
                            doStuff(null);
                        }catch(NullPointerException npe) {
                                System.out.println("-catch-");
                        }
                }
          }
```

What is the result?

a) –catch--finally—dostuff

b) –catch

c) –finally—catch

d) –finally-dostuff--catch

Answer: c

83. Given the code fragment:

```
final list<String>= new CopyWriteArrayList<> ( ) ;
```

```
final AtomicInteger ai = new AtomicInteger (0) ;
final Cyclicbarrier barrier = newCyclicBarrier (2, new Runnable () {
        public void run ( ) {System.out.println(list);  }
});
 Runnable r = new Runnable ( ) {
        public void run ( ) {
try {
      Thread. sleep (1000 * ai. incrementAndGet ( ) ) ;
       list. add ("X");
                 barrier. await ( ) ;
           }  catch (Exception ex) {
           }
        }
};
new Thread (r) . start ( ) ;
new Thread (r) . start ( ) ;
new Thread (r) . start ( ) ;
new Thread (r) . start ( ) ;
```

What is the result ?

a) [X][X, X][X, X, X][X, X, X, X]

b) [X, X]

c) [X][X, X][X, X, X]

d) [X, X][X, X, X, X]

Answer: a

84. Which two are elements of a singleton class? (Choose two.)

a) a transient reference to point to the single instance

b) a public method to instantiate the single instance

c) a public static method to return a copy of the singleton reference

d) a private constructor to the class

e) a public reference to point to the single instance

Answer: b,d

85. Which two methods from the java.util.stream.Stream interface perform a reduction operation? (Choose two.)

a) count ()

b) collect ()

c) distinct ()

d) peek ()

e) filter ()

Answer: a, b

86. Given the code fragment:

List<String> empDetails = Arrays.asList("100, Robin, HR", "200, Mary, AdminServices", "101, Peter, HR");

empDetails.stream()

.filter(s-> s.contains("1"))

.sorted()

.f orEach(System.out::println); //line n1

What is the result?

a) 100, Robin, HR101, Peter, HR

b) A compilation error occurs at line n1.

c) 100, Robin, HR101, Peter, HR200, Mary, AdminServices

d) 100, Robin, HR200, Mary, AdminServices101, Peter, HR

Answer: a

87. Given the code fragment:

List<String> str = Arrays.asList ("my", "pen", "is", "your', "pen"); Predicate<String> test = s ->

{

int i = 0;

boolean result = s.contains ("pen");

System.out.print(i++) + ":"); return result;

};

str.stream()

.filter(test)

.findFirst()

.i fPresent(System.out ::print);

What is the result?

a) 0 : 0 : pen

b) 0 : 1 : pen

c) 0 : 0 : 0 : 0 : 0 : pen

d) 0 : 1 : 2 : 3 : 4 :

e) A compilation error occurs.

Answer: a

88. Given the code fragment:

List<Integer> nums = Arrays.asList (10, 20, 8): System.out.println (

//line n1

); Which code fragment must be inserted at line n1 to enable the code to print the maximum number in the nums list?

a) nums.stream().max(Comparator.comparing(a -> a)).get()

b) nums.stream().max(Integer : : max).get()

c) nums.stream().max()

d) nums.stream().map(a -> a).max()

Answer: a

89. Given the code fragment:

Connection conn = DriveManager.getConnection(dbURL, userName, passWord);

String query = “SELECT id FROM Employee”;

try (Statement stmt = conn.createStatement()) {

ResultSet rs = stmt.executeQuery(query);

stmt.executeQuery(“SELECT id FROM Customer”);

while (rs.next()) {

```
//process the results
System.out.println("Employee ID: "+ rs.getInt("id"));
}
} catch (Exception e) {
System.out.println ("Error");
}
```

Assume that:

The required database driver is configured in the classpath.

The appropriate database is accessible with the dbURL, userName, and passWord exists.

The Employee and Customer tables are available and each table has id column with a few records and the SQL queries are valid.

What is the result of compiling and executing this code fragment?

a) The program prints employee IDs.

b) The program prints customer IDs.

c) The program prints Error.

d) compilation fails on line 13.

Answer: c

90. Given the definition of the Vehicle class:

```
Class Vehhicle {
int distance; //line n1 Vehicle (int x) {
this distance = x;
}
public void increSpeed(int time) { //line n2 int timeTravel = time; //line n3
class Car { int value = 0;
public void speed () {
value = distance /timeTravel;
System.out.println ("Velocity with new speed"+value+"kmph");
}
}
new Car().speed();
```

}

}

and this code fragment: Vehicle v = new Vehicle (100); v.increSpeed(60);

What is the result?

a) Velocity with new speed

b) A compilation error occurs at line n1.

c) A compilation error occurs at line n2.

d) A compilation error occurs at line n3.

Answer: a

91. Given the code fragment:

Map<Integer, String> books = new TreeMap<>(); books.put (1007, “A”);

books.put (1002, “C”);

books.put (1001, “B”);

books.put (1003, “B”); System.out.println (books);

What is the result?

a) {1007 = A, 1002 = C, 1001 = B, 1003 = B}

b) {1001 = B, 1002 = C, 1003 = B, 1007 = A}

c) {1002 = C, 1003 = B, 1007 = A}

d) {1007 = A, 1001 = B, 1003 = B, 1002 = C}

Answer: b

92. Given:

class Vehicle { int vno;

String name;

public Vehicle (int vno, String name) { this.vno = vno,;

this.name = name;

}

public String toString () { return vno + “:” + name;

}

}

and this code fragment:

Set<Vehicle> vehicles = new TreeSet <> (); vehicles.add(new Vehicle (10123, “Ford”));

vehicles.add(new Vehicle (10124, “BMW”)); System.out.println(vehicles);

What is the result?

a) 10123 Ford10124 BMW

b) 10124 BMW10123 Ford

c) A compilation error occurs.

d) A ClassCastException is thrown at run time.

Answer: d

93. Given the records from the STUDENT table:

```
public static void main (String() args) throws SQLException {
//code to load and register valid jdbc driver go here
Connection con = DriverManager.getconnection (URI,, username, password) ;
Statement st = con.createStatement (ResultSet.TYPE_SCROLL_INSENSITIVE,
Resultset .CONCUR_UPDATABLE) ;
st.execute ("SELECT FROM student") ;
ResultSet rs = st.getResultSet() ;
rs. absolute (3) ;
rs . moveToInsertRow ( ) ;
rs.updateInt (1, 113) ;
rs . updateString (2, "Jannet") ;
rs. updateString (3, "jannet @uni.com") ;

rs. updateRow ( ) ;
rs. refreshRow ;
System. out. println (rs.getInt (1) + “  :   ”+ rs.getString(2) + “  :   ”+ rs.getString
(3));
        }
```

Assume that the URL, username, and password are valid. What is the result?

a) The STUDENT table is not updated and the program prints: 114 : John : john@uni.com

b) The STUDENT table is updated with the record: 113 : Jannet : jannet@uni.comand the program prints: 114 : John : john@uni.com

c) The STUDENT table is updated with the record: 113 : Jannet : jannet@uni.comand the program prints:113 : Jannet : jannet@uni.com

d) A SQLException is thrown at run time.

Answer: a

94. Given:

class Student {

String course, name, city;

public Student (String name, String course, String city) { this.course = course; this.name = name; this.city = city;

}

public String toString() {

return course + ":" + name + ":" + city;

}

and the code fragment: List<Student> stds = Arrays.asList(

new Student ("Jessy", "Java ME", "Chicago"), new Student ("Helen", "Java EE", "Houston"),

new Student ("Mark", "Java ME", "Chicago")); stds.stream()

.collect(Collectors.groupingBy(Student::getCourse))

.f orEach(src, res) -> System.out.println(scr)); What is the result?

a) [Java EE: Helen:Houston][Java ME: Jessy:Chicago, Java ME: Mark:Chicago]

b) Java EEJava ME

c) [Java ME: Jessy:Chicago, Java ME: Mark:Chicago] [Java EE: Helen:Houston]

d) A compilation error occurs.

Answer: b

95. Given the code fragment:

List<Integer> codes = Arrays.asList (10, 20); UnaryOperator<Double> uo = s -> s +10.0; codes.replaceAll(uo);

codes.forEach(c -> System.out.println(c)); What is the result?

a) 20.030.0

b) 1020

c) A compilation error occurs.

d) A NumberFormatException is thrown at run time.

Answer: c

96. Assume customers.txt is accessible and contains multiple lines. Which code fragment prints the contents of the customers.txt file?

a) Stream<String> stream = Files.find (Paths.get ("customers.txt")); stream.forEach((String c) -> System.out.println(c));

b) Stream<Path> stream = Files.find (Paths.get ("customers.txt")); stream.forEach(c) -> System.out.println(c));

c) Stream<Path> stream = Files.list (Paths.get ("customers.txt")); stream.forEach(c) -> System.out.println(c));

d) Stream<String> lines = Files.lines (Paths.get ("customers.txt")); lines.forEach(c) -> System.out.println(c));

Answer: a

97. For which three objects must a vendor provide implementations in its JDBC driver? (Choose three.)

a) Time

b) Date

c) Statement

d) ResultSet

e) Connection

f) SQLException

g) DriverManager

Answer: c,d,e

98. Given:

interface Rideable {Car getCar (String name); } class Car {

private String name; public Car (String name) { this.name = name;

}

}

Which code fragment creates an instance of Car?

a) Car auto = Car (“MyCar”): : new;

b) Car auto = Car : : new;Car vehicle = auto : : getCar(“MyCar”);

c) Rideable rider = Car : : new;Car vehicle = rider.getCar(“MyCar”);

d) Car vehicle = Rideable : : new : : getCar(“MyCar”);

Answer: c

99. Given the definition of the Vehicle class: class Vehicle {

String name;

void setName (String name) { this.name = name;

}

String getName() { return name;

}

}

Which action encapsulates the Vehicle class?

a) Make the Vehicle class public.

b) Make the name variable public.

c) Make the setName method public.

d) Make the name variable private.

e) Make the setName method private.

f) Make the getName method private.

Answer: d

100. Given the code fragment:

try{

properties prop = new properties ( ) ;

prop. put ("user", userName) ;

prop. put ("password", passWord) ;

```
Connection conn = DriverManager . getconnection (dbURL, prop);
if (conn!= null) {
System. out. print ( "Connection Established") ;
} catch (Exception e)
                    System. out .print (e) ;
}
```

and the information:

The required database driver is configured in the classpath.

The appropriate database is accessible with the dbURL, username, and passWord exists. What is the result?

a) A ClassNotFoundException is thrown at runtime.

b) The program prints nothing.

c) The program prints Connection Established.

d) A SQLException is thrown at runtime.

Answer: c

101. Given the code fragments:

```
public class Book implements Comparator<Book> { String name;
double price; public Book () {}
public Book(String name, double price) { this.name = name;
this.price = price;
}
public int compare(Book b1, Book b2) { return b1.name.compareTo(b2.name);
}
public String toString() { return name + ":" + price;
}
}
```

and

```
List<Book>books = Arrays.asList (new Book ("Beginning with Java", 2), new book ("A
Guide to Java Tour", 3));
Collections.sort(books, new Book()); System.out.print(books);
```

What is the result?

a) [A Guide to Java Tour:3.0, Beginning with Java:2.0]

b) [Beginning with Java:2, A Guide to Java Tour:3]

c) A compilation error occurs because the Book class does not override the abstract method compareTo().

d) An Exception is thrown at run time.

Answer: a

102. Given the code fragment:

Stream<Path> files = Files.walk(Paths.get(System.getProperty("user.home"))); files.forEach

(fName -> { //line n1

try {

Path aPath = fName.toAbsolutePath(); //line n2 System.out.println(fName + ":"

+ Files.readAttributes(aPath, Basic.File.Attributes.class).creationTime ());

} catch (IOException ex) { ex.printStackTrace(); });

What is the result?

a) All files and directories under the home directory are listed along with their attributes.

b) A compilation error occurs at line n1.

c) The files in the home directory are listed along with their attributes.

d) A compilation error occurs at line n2.

Answer: a

103. Which statement is true about java.util.stream.Stream?

a) A stream cannot be consumed more than once.

b) The execution mode of streams can be changed during processing.

c) Streams are intended to modify the source data.

d) A parallel stream is always faster than an equivalent sequential stream.

Answer: b

104. Given the content:

Messaages

MessagesBundle . properties file:

```
username = Enter User Name
password = Enter password
```

MessagesBundle_fr_ FR.properties file:

```
username = Entrez le nom d'utilisateur
password = Entrez le mot de passe
```

and the code fragment:

```
locale currentLocale = new Locale.Builder().setRegion("FR").setLanguage("fr").build() ;
ResourceBundIe messages = ResourceBundle .getBundle ("MessagesBundIe", currentLocale) ;
Enumeration<String>names = messages.getKeys() ;
while (names. hasMoreElements ()) {
String key= names.nextElement();
String name = messages .getString (key) ;
System.out.println(key + " = " + name) ;
        }
```

What is the result?

a) username = Entrez le nom d'utilisateur password = Entrez le mot de passe

b) username = Enter User Name password = Enter Password

c) A compilation error occurs.

d) The program prints nothing.

Answer: a

105. Given the code fragment:

```
public static void main (String [ ] args) throws
  IOException
  { BufferReader br = new BufferReader (new
   InputStreamReader (System. in)) ; System. out. print
```

("Enter GDP: ");

//line 1

Which code fragment, when inserted at line 1 , enables the code to read

a) the GDP from the user?

b) int GDP = Integer . parseInt (br.readline()) ;

c) int GDP = br.read();

d) int GDP = br.nextInt() ;

e) int GDP = Integer . parse Int (br . next ( )) ;

Answer: a

106. Given the code fragment: UnaryOperator<Integer> uo1 = s -> s*2; line n1

List<Double> loanValues = Arrays.asList(1000.0, 2000.0); loanValues.stream()

.filter(lv -> lv >= 1500)

.map(lv -> uo1.apply(lv))

.forEach(s -> System.out.print(s + " ")); What is the result?

a) 4000.0

b) 4000

c) A compilation error occurs at line n1.

d) A compilation error occurs at line n2.

Answer: d

107. Given the code fragment:

// line n1

System.out.println(iP) ;

Which code fragment, when inserted at line n1, enables the code to print /First.txt?

a) Path iP = new Paths ("/First.txt");

b) Path iP = Paths.toPath ("/First.txt");

c) Path iP = new Path ("/First.txt");

d) Path iP = Paths.get ("/", "First.txt");

Answer: d

108. Given:

```
public interface Moveable<Integer> {
public default void walk (Integer distance) {System.out.println("Walking");) public void run(Integer distance);
}
```

Which statement is true?

a) Moveable can be used as below:Moveable<Integer> animal = n - > System.out.println("Running" + n); animal.run(100);animal.walk(20);

b) Moveable can be used as below: Moveable<Integer> animal = n - > n + 10; animal.run(100);animal.walk(20);

c) Moveable can be used as below:Moveable animal = (Integer n) - > System.out.println(n); animal.run(100);Moveable.walk(20);

d) Movable cannot be used in a lambda expression.

Answer: a

109. Given that version.txt is accessible and contains: 1234567890

and given the code fragment:

```
try (FileInputStream fis = new FileInputStream ("version. txt") ;
InputStreamReader isr = new InputStreamReader (fis) ;
BufferedReader br = new BufferedReader (isr ) ; ) {
    if (br.markSupported())   {
        System.out.print ((char) br.read()) ;
         br.mark(2);
         System.out.print( (char) br.read () );
      }
  }catch (Exception e) {
        e.printStackTrace();
 }
```

What is the result?

a) 121

b) 122

c) 135

d) The program prints nothing.

Answer: b

110. Given the structure of the STUDENT table: Student (id INTEGER, name VARCHAR)

Given:

public class Test {

static Connection newConnection =null;

public static Connection get DBConnection () throws SQLException { try (Connection con = DriveManager.getConnection(URL, username, password)) {

newConnection = con;

}

return newConnection;

}

public static void main (String [] args) throws SQLException { get DBConnection ();

Statement st = newConnection.createStatement(); st.executeUpdate("INSERT INTO student VALUES (102, 'Kelvin')");

}

}

Assume that:

The required database driver is configured in the classpath.

The appropriate database is accessible with the URL, userName, and passWord exists. The SQL query is valid.

What is the result?

a) The program executes successfully and the STUDENT table is updated with one record.

b) The program executes successfully and the STUDENT table is NOT updated with any record.

c) A SQLException is thrown as runtime.

d) A NullPointerException is thrown as runtime.

Answer: c

111. Given:

```
class Student {
String course, name, city;
public Student (String name, String course, String city) { this.course = course; this.name = name;
this.city = city;
}
public String toString() {
return course + ":" + name + ":" + city;
}
```

and the code fragment: List<Student> stds = Arrays.asList(

```
new Student ("Jessy", "Java ME", "Chicago"), new Student ("Helen", "Java EE", "Houston"),
new Student ("Mark", "Java ME", "Chicago")); stds.stream()
.collect(Collectors.groupingBy(Student::getCourse))
.f orEach(src, res) -> System.out.println(scr));
```

What is the result?

a) [Java EE: Helen:Houston][Java ME: Jessy:Chicago, Java ME: Mark:Chicago]

b) Java EEJava ME

c) [Java ME: Jessy:Chicago, Java ME: Mark:Chicago] [Java EE: Helen:Houston]

d) A compilation error occurs.

Answer: b

112. Given:

```
class FuelNotAvailException extends Exception { } class Vehicle {
void ride() throws FuelNotAvailException { //line n1 System.out.println("Happy Journey!");
}
}
class SolarVehicle extends Vehicle {
public void ride () throws Exception { //line n2 super ride ();
}
}
```

and the code fragment:

public static void main (String[] args) throws FuelNotAvailException, Exception

{

Vehicle v = new SolarVehicle (); v.ride();

}

Which modification enables the code fragment to print Happy Journey!?

a) Replace line n1 with public void ride() throws FuelNotAvailException {

b) Replace line n1 with protected void ride() throws Exception {

c) Replace line n2 with void ride() throws Exception {

d) Replace line n2 with private void ride() throws FuelNotAvailException {

Answer: b

113. Given the code fragments:

class Caller implements Callable<String> { String str;

public Caller (String s) {this.str=s;}

public String call()throws Exception { return str.concat ("Caller");}

}

class Runner implements Runnable { String str;

public Runner (String s) {this.str=s;}

public void run () { System.out.println (str.concat ("Runner"));}

}

and

public static void main (String[] args) InterruptedException, ExecutionException

{

ExecutorService es = Executors.newFixedThreadPool(2); Future f1 = es.submit (new Caller ("Call"));

Future f2 = es.submit (new Runner ("Run")); String str1 = (String) f1.get();

String str2 = (String) f2.get(); //line n1 System.out.println(str1+ ":" + str2);

}

What is the result?

a) The program prints: Run RunnerCall Caller : nullAnd the program does not terminate.

b) The program terminates after printing: Run RunnerCall Caller : Run

c) A compilation error occurs at line n1.

d) An Execution is thrown at run time.

Answer: a

114. Given the code fragment:

```
Deque<Integer> nums = new ArrayDeque<> ();
nums . add (1000) ;
nums . push (2000) ;
nums . add (3000) ;
nums . push (4000) :
Integer i1 =  nums. remove ( ) ;
Integer i2 = nums.pop ( ) ;
System.out.println( (i1 + " : " + i2);
```

What is the result?

a) 4000 : 2000

b) 4000 : 1000

c) 1000 : 4000

d) 1000 : 2000

Answer: b

115. Given the code fragment:

```
public void recDelete (String dirName) throws IOException { File [ ] listOfFiles = new File
(dirName) .listFiles();
if (listOfFiles ! = null && listOfFiles.length >0) {
for (File aFile : listOfFiles) { if (aFile.isDirectory ()) {
recDelete (aFile.getAbsolutePath ());
} else {
if (aFile.getName ().endsWith (".class")) aFile.delete ();
}
}
}
```

}

Assume that Projects contains subdirectories that contain .class files and is passed as an argument to the recDelete () method when it is invoked.

What is the result?

a) The method deletes all the .class files in the Projects directory and its subdirectories.

b) The method deletes the .class files of the Projects directory only.

c) The method executes and does not make any changes to the Projects directory.

d) The method throws an IOException.

Answer: a

116. Given:

```
abstract class Shape {
Shape ( ) { System.out.println ("Shape"); }
protected void area ( ) { System.out.println ("Shape"); } 4. }
class Square extends Shape {
int side;
Square int side {
/* insert code here */
 this.side = side;
 }
 public void area ( ) { System.out.println ("Square"); }
 }
 class Rectangle extends Square {
 int len, br;
 Rectangle (int x, int y) {
 /* insert code here */
 len = x, br = y;
 }
 void area ( ) { System.out.println ("Rectangle"); }
 }
```

Which two modifications enable the code to compile? (Choose two.)

a) At line 1, remove abstract

b) At line 9, insert super ( );

c) At line 12, remove public

d) At line 17, insert super (x);

e) At line 17, insert super (); super.side = x;

f) At line 20, use public void area ( ) {

Answer: d, f

117. Given the code fragment:

class CallerThread implements Callable<String> { String str;

public CallerThread(String s) {this.str=s;} public String call() throws Exception { return str.concat("Call");

}

}

and

public static void main (String[] args) throws InterruptedException, ExecutionException

{

ExecutorService es = Executors.newFixedThreadPool(4); //line n1 Future f1 = es.submit (newCallerThread("Call"));

String str = f1.get().toString(); System.out.println(str);

}

Which statement is true?

a) The program prints Call Call and terminates.

b) The program prints Call Call and does not terminate.

c) A compilation error occurs at line n1.

d) An ExecutionException is thrown at run time.

Answer: b

118. Given the code fragment:

String str = "Java is a programming language"; ToIntFunction<String> indexVal = str: : indexOf; //line n1 int x = indexVal.applyAsInt("Java"); //line n2

System.out.println(x); What is the result?

a) 1

b) A compilation error occurs at line n1.

c) A compilation error occurs at line n2.

Answer: a

119. Which two statements are true about localizing an application? (Choose two.)

a) Support for new regional languages does not require recompilation of the code.

b) Textual elements (messages and GUI labels) are hard-coded in the code.

c) Language and region-specific programs are created using localized data.

d) Resource bundle files include data and currency information.

e) Language codes use lowercase letters and region codes use uppercase letters.

Answer: a, e

120. Given the code fragment:

```
        try{
Connection conn = DriverManager . getconnection (dbURL, userName, passWord) ;
String query = "SELECT * FROM Employee WHERE ID = 110" ;
Statement stmt ( ) = conn.createStatement() ;
ResultSet rs = stmt. executequery (query) ;
System. out . printin ( "Employee ID: " + rs.get("ID")) ;
        }catch (Exception se) {
System. out . println ( "Error:" ) ;
        }
```

Assume that:

The required database driver is configured in the classpath.

The appropriate database is accessible with the dbURL, userName, and passWord exists The Employee table has a column ID of type integer and the SQL query matches one record. What is the result?

a) Compilation fails at line 14.

b) Compilation fails at line 15.

c) The code prints the employee ID.

d) The code prints Error.

Answer: a

121. Given the code fragment:

List<String> codes = Arrays.asList ("DOC", "MPEG", "JPEG"); codes.forEach (c -> System.out.print(c + " "));

String fmt = codes.stream()

.filter (s-> s.contains ("PEG"))

.r educe((s, t) -> s + t).get(); System.out.println("\n" + fmt); What is the result?

a) DOC MPEG JPEG MPEGJPEG

b) DOC MPEG MPEGJPEG MPEGMPEGJPEG

c) MPEGJPEG MPEGJPEG

d) The order of the output is unpredictable.

Answer: a

122. Given:

class UserException extends Exception { }

class AgeOutOfLimitException extends UserException { } and the code fragment:

class App {

public void doRegister(String name, int age) throws UserException, AgeOutOfLimitException {

if (name.length () < 6) {

throw new UserException ();

} else if (age >= 60) {

throw new AgeOutOfLimitException ();

System.out.println("User is registered.");

}

}

public static void main(String[ ] args) throws UserException { App t = new App ();

a) t.d oRegister("Mathew", 60);}}What is the result?

b) User is registered.

c) An AgeOutOfLimitException is thrown.

d) A UserException is thrown.

e) A compilation error occurs in the main method.

Answer: b

123. Which statement is true about the single abstract method of the java.util.function.Function interface?

a) It accepts one argument and returns void.

b) It accepts one argument and returns boolean.

c) It accepts one argument and always produces a result of the same type as the argument.

d) It accepts an argument and produces a result of any data type.

Answer: d

124. Given that course.txt is accessible and contains:

Course : : Java

and given the code fragment:

```
public static void main (String[ ] args) { int i;
char c;
try (FileInputStream fis = new FileInputStream ("course.txt"); InputStreamReader isr = new
InputStreamReader(fis);) { while (isr.ready()) { //line n1
isr.skip(2);
i = isr.read (); c = (char) i;
System.out.print(c);
}
} catch (Exception e) { e.printStackTrace();
}
}
```

What is the result?

a) ur :: va

b) ueJa

c) The program prints nothing.

d) A compilation error occurs at line n1.

Answer: b

125. Given the code fragment:

Path path1 = Paths.get("/app/./sys/"); Path res1 = path1.resolve("log");

Path path2 = Paths.get("/server/exe/"); Path res1 = path1.resolve("/readme/"); System.out.println(res1);

System.out.println(res2);

What is the result?

a) /app/sys/log/readme/server/exe

b) /app/log/sys/server/exe/readme

c) /app/./sys/log/readme

d) /app/./sys/log/server/exe/readme

Answer: c

126. Given:

IntStream stream = IntStream.of (1,2,3); IntFunction<Integer> inFu= x -> y -> x*y; //line n1

IntStream newStream = stream.map(inFu.apply(10)); //line n2 newStream.forEach(System.output::print);

Which modification enables the code fragment to compile?

a) Replace line n1 with: IntFunction<UnaryOperator> inFu = x -> y -> x*y;

b) Replace line n1 with: IntFunction<IntUnaryOperator> inFu = x -> y -> x*y;

c) Replace line n1 with: BiFunction<IntUnaryOperator> inFu = x -> y -> x*y;

d) Replace line n2 with:IntStream newStream = stream.map(inFu.applyAsInt (10));

Answer: b

127. Given:

class MyClass implements AutoCloseable {
int test;

```
public void close ( ) { }
public MyClass copyObject ( ) {return this; }
}
```

What is the result?

a) An exception is thrown at line n2.

b) 100

c) A compilation error occurs because the try block is declared without a catch or finally block.

d) A compilation error occurs at line n1.

Answer: d

128. Given:

```
public class Test<T> { private T t;
public T get () { return t;
}
public void set (T t) { this.t = t;
}
public static void main (String args [ ] ) { Test<String> type = new Test<>();
Test type 1 = new Test (); //line n1 type.set("Java");
type1.set(100); //line n2 System.out.print(type.get() + " " + type1.get());
}
}
```

What is the result?

a) Java 100

b) java.lang.string@<hashcode>java.lang.Integer@<hashcode>

c) A compilation error occur

d) To rectify it, replace line n1 with: Test<Integer> type1 = new Test<>();

e) A compilation error occur

f) To rectify it, replace line n2 with: type1.set (Integer(100));

Answer: a

129. Given:

```
public final class IceCream { public void prepare() {}
}
public class Cake {
public final void bake(int min, int temp) {} public void mix() {}
}
public class Shop {
private Cake c = new Cake (); private final double discount = 0.25;
public void makeReady () { c.bake(10, 120); }
}
public class Bread extends Cake {
public void bake(int minutes, int temperature) {} public void addToppings() {}
}
```

Which statement is true?

a) A compilation error occurs in IceCream.

b) A compilation error occurs in Cake.

c) A compilation error occurs in Shop.

d) A compilation error occurs in Bread

e) All classes compile successfully.

Answer: d

130. Given the code fragments:

```
    void doStuff() throws ArithmeticException,
    NumberFormatException,
    Exception
    {
            if (Math.random() >-1 throw new Exception (“Try
    again”);
```

and

```
try {
        doStuff ( ):
 } catch (ArithmeticException |
   NumberFormatException | Exception
    e)
 {
        System.out.println (e.getMessage()); }
 catch (Exception e) {
        System.out.println (e.getMessage()); }
  }
```

Which modification enables the code to print Try again?

a) Comment the lines 28, 29 and 30.

b) Replace line 26 with:} catch (Exception | ArithmeticException | NumberFormatException e) {

c) Replace line 26 with:} catch (ArithmeticException | NumberFormatException e) {

d) Replace line 27 with: throw e;

Answer: c

131. Given:

```
class ImageScanner implements AutoCloseable { public void close () throws Exception {
System.out.print ("Scanner closed.");
}
public void scanImage () throws Exception { System.out.print ("Scan.");
throw new Exception("Unable to scan.");
}
}
class ImagePrinter implements AutoCloseable { public void close () throws Exception {
System.out.print ("Printer closed.");
}
public void printImage () {System.out.print("Print."); }
}
```

and this code fragment:

```
try (ImageScanner ir = new ImageScanner(); ImagePrinter iw = new ImagePrinter()) {
ir.scanImage();
iw.printImage();
} catch (Exception e) { System.out.print(e.getMessage());
}
```

What is the result?

a) Scan.Printer close

b) Scanner close

c) Unable to scan.

d) Scan.Scanner close

e) Unable to scan.

f) Sca

Answer: a

132. Given the code fragments:

```
public class Video {
public void play ( ) throws IOException {
System. out . print ("Video played. ")
                    }
          }
public class Game extends Video {
public void play ( ) throws Exception {
super . play ( ) ;
System. out . print ("Game played. ")
}
 }
```

and

```
try {
     new Game ( ) . play ( ) ;
}catch (Exception e) {
System. out . print (e .getCiass ( ) ) ;
```

}

What is the result?

a) Video played.Game played.

b) A compilation error occurs.

c) class java.lang.Exception

d) class java.io.IOException

Answer: c

133. Which action can be used to load a database driver by using JDBC3.0?

a) Add the driver class to the META-INF/services folder of the JAR file.

b) Include the JDBC driver class in a jdbc.properties file.

c) Use the java.lang.Class.forName method to load the driver class.

d) Use the DriverManager.getDriver method to load the driver class.

Answer: c

134. Given that /green.txt and /colors/yellow.txt are accessible, and the code fragment:

Path source = Paths.get("/green.txt);

Path target = Paths.get("/colors/yellow.txt);

Files.move(source, target, StandardCopyOption.ATOMIC_MOVE); Files.delete(source);

Which statement is true?

a) The green.txt file content is replaced by the yellow.txt file content and the yellow.txt file is deleted.

b) The yellow.txt file content is replaced by the green.txt file content and an exception is thrown.

c) The file green.txt is moved to the /colors directory.

d) A FileAlreadyExistsException is thrown at runtime.

Answer: d

135. Given the code fragment:

ZonedDateTime depart = ZonedDateTime.of(2015, 1, 15, 3, 0, 0, 0, ZoneID.of("UTC7"));

ZonedDateTime arrive = ZonedDateTime.of(2015, 1, 15, 9, 0, 0, 0, ZoneID.of("UTC5"));

long hrs = ChronoUnit.HOURS.between(depart, arrive); //line n1 System.out.println("Travel time is" + hrs + "hours");

What is the result?

a) Travel time is 4 hours

b) Travel time is 6 hours

c) Travel time is 8 hours

d) An exception is thrown at line n1.

Answer: a

136. Given the content Of / resourses/Message . properties:

welcome 1= "Good day! "

and given the code fragment:

Properties prop = new Properties ( ) ;

FileInputStream fis = new FileInputStream

('/ resources/Message . properties") ; prop. load (f is) ;

System. out . println (prop. getProperty ("welcomel)) ;

System. out . println (prop. getProperty ("welcome2" , "Test")); // line n1

System. out . println (prop. getProperty ("welcome3")) ;

What is the result?

a) Good day!

Test

followed by an Exception stack trace

b) Good day!

followed by an Exception stack trace

c) Good day! Test null

d) A compilation error occurs at line nl.

Answer: c

137. Given:

class ImageScanner implements AutoCloseab1e { public

```
void close ( ) throws Exception {
        System. out . print ("Scanner closed. 't) ;
}
public void scanlmage ( ) throws Exception {
      System. out . print ("Scan." ) ;
      throw new Exception ("Unable to scan.

class Imageprinter implements AutoCloseab1e { public
    void close ( ) throws Exception {
       System. out . print ("Printer closed. ;
    }
    public void print Image ( ) {   System. out . printImage ("Print
```

and this code fragment:

```
try (ImageScanner ir = new ImageScanner ( ) ;  ImagePrinter
          iw = new ImagePrinter())
    ir . scan Image ( ) ; iw. print Image ( ) ;
} catch (Exception e )
     System. out . print (e. getMessage ( ) ) ;
}
```

What is the result?

a) Scan. Printer closed. Scanner closed. Unable to scan.

b) Scan. Scanner closed. Printer closed. Unable to scan.

c) Scan. Unable to scan.

d) Scan. Unable to scan. Scanner closed.

Answer: a

138. Given the structure of the STUDENT table:

Student (id INTEGER, name VARCHAR)

Given:

```
public class Test
    static Connection newConnection =null;
     public static Connection get DBConnection ( ) throws
     SQLException {
            try (Connection con =
                  DriveManager . getConnection (URL, username,
                    password) )

                    { newConnection = con;
```

What is the result of executing the following application? (Choose all that apply.)

```
import java. util. concurrent.*;
import java. util.stream.*;
public class BabyPandaBathManager {
     public static void await(CyclicBarrier cb) {
          try {
              cb. await();
          }catch (InterruptedException I BrokenBarrierException e) {
               // Handle exception
          }
      }
public static void main(String[] args) {
     final CyclicBarrier cb = new CyclicBarrier(3, ( )->

System. out. println("Clean! "));// u1
          Executorservice service = Executors . newScheduledThreadPool(2) ;
          IntStream.iterate(1,i-> 1) // u2
   . limit(12)
```

```
    .forEach(i-> service. submit( // u3
        ()-> await(cb))); // u4
        service. shutdown();
    }
}
```

a) It outputs Clean! at least once.

b) It outputs Clean! four times.

c) The code will not compile because of line ul.

d) The code will not compile because of line u2.

e) The code will not compile because of line u3.

f) The code will not compile because of line u4.

g) It compiles but throws an exception at runtime.

h) It compiles but waits forever at runtime.

Answer: h

139.What is the result of the following program?

```
public abstract class Message {
    public String recipient;
    public abstract final void sendMessage();
    public static void main(StringC] args) {
        Message m = new TextMessage();
        m. recipient = "1234567890";
        m. sendMessage() ;
}
static class TextMessage extends Message {
    public final void sendMessage() {
        System. out. println( "Text message to" + recipient);
    }}}
```

a) Text message to null.

b) Text message to 1234567890.

c) A compiler error occurs on line 1.

d) A compiler error occurs on line 3.

e) A compiler error occurs on line 7.

f) A compiler error occurs on another line.

Answer: d

140. What is the result of executing the following code? (Choose all that apply.)

```
import java.io.*
public class Tail {}
public class Bird implements Serializable {
            private String name;
            private transient int age;
            private Tail tail;

public String getName() { return name;}
public Tail getTai1() { return tail;}
public void setName(String name) { this. name = name; }
public void setTai1(Tail tail) { this. tail =  tail;
public int getAge() { return age;}
public void setAge(int age) { this. age = age; }

public static void main (String[]args) {
    try(InputStream is = new ObjectlnputStream(
         new Bufferedlnputstream(new
FileInputStream( "birds.dat")))) {
          Bird bird = is. readObject();
          }
      }
}
```

a) It compiles and runs without issue.

b) The code will not compile because of line 3.

c) The code will not compile because of line 5.

d) The code will not compile because of lines 16—17.

e) The code will not compile because of line 18.

f) It compiles but throws an exception at runtime.

Answer: d,e

141. What is the result of the following class?

```
public class Box<T> {
    T value;

      public Box(T value) {
          this. value = value;
      }
      public T getVa1ue() {
      return value;
      }
      public static void main(String[] args) {
          Box<String> one = new Box<String>("a string");
          Box<Integer> two = new Box<>(123);
          System. out . print (one. getVa1ue( ) ) ;
          System. out . print( two. getVa1ue( ) ) ;
        }}
```

a) Compiler error on line 1.

b) Compiler error on line 2.

c) Compiler error on line 11.

d) Compiler error on line 12.

e) a string123

f) An exception is thrown.

Answer: e

142. What is the result of executing the following code snippet?

```
List<Integer> source = new ArrayList<>(Arrays.asList(1,2,3,4));
List<Integer> fish = new CopyOnWriteArrayList<>(source);
List<Integer> mammals = Collections. synchronizedList(source);
Set<Integer> birds = new ConcurrentSkipListSet<>();
birds. addA11 (source) ;

synchronized(new Integer(10)) {
    for(Integer f: fish) fish.add(4); // cl
    for(Integer m: mammals) mammals.add(4); // c2
    for(Integer b: birds) birds. add(S); // c3
    System. out.println(fish.size()+"
"+birds . size ( ) );
}
```

a) It outputs 4 8 5.

b) It outputs 8 4 5.

c) It outputs 8 8 8.

d) The code does not compile.

e) It compiles but throws an exception at runtime on line cl.

f) It compiles but throws an exception at runtime on line c2.

g) It compiles but throws an exception at runtime on line c3.

h) It compiles but enters an infinite loop at runtime.

Answer: f

143. What changes would need to be made to make the following immutable object pattern correct? (Choose all that apply.)

```
import java. util.List;
public class Duck {
    private String name;
```

```
    private List<Duck> ducklings;
    public Duck(String name, List<Duck> ducklings) {
        this . name = name;
        this . ducklings = new ArrayList<Duck>(ducklings);
    }
     public String getName() { return name;}
     public List<Duck> getDucklings() { return ducklings;}
     public String hasDucklings(Predicate<Duck> p) {
        return p.test(this) ? "Quack Quack": "";
     }
}
```

a) None, the immutable object pattern is properly implemented.

b) Mark name and ducklings final.

c) Mark the Duck class final.

d) Have Duck implement the Immutable interface.

e) Remove the hasDucklings() method since any lambda expressions

f) passed to it could modify the Duck object.

g) Replace the getDucklings( ) with a method (or methods) that do not

h) give the caller direct access to the List<Duck> ducklings.

i) Change the type of List<Duck> to be List<Object>.

Answer: b,c,f

144. Assuming the current directory /bats/day and all of the files and directories referenced here exist and are available within the file system, what is the result of executing the following code?

```
Path pathl = Paths.get( "/bats/night" , " . ./") . resolve (Paths . get(
" ./sleep.txt")) . normalize(); Path path2 = new
File(".. / sleep .txt") .toPath() . toRea1Path() ;
System.out.print(Fi1es.isSameFi1e(path1,path2)); System. out. print("
"+pathl.equals ( path2) ) ;
```

a) true true

b) false false

c) true false

d) false true

e) The code does not compile.

f) The code compiles but throws an exception at runtime.

Answer: a

145. What statements are true about the following code? (Choose all that apply.)

```
public class Tail{}
    public class Animal {
  public String name;
}
public class Canine extends Animal {
   public Tail tail;
}
public class Wolf extends Canine {}
```

a) Wolf has-a name.

b) Wolf has-a Tail.

c) Wolf is-a Tail.

d) Wolf is-a Animal.

e) Canine is-a Wolf.

f) Animal has-a Tail.

Answer: a, b, d

146. Which of the following can fill in the blank? (Choose all that apply.)

```
public void stmt(Connection conn, int a) throws SQLException {
  Statement stmt = conn. createStatement(a,
_________________________);
```

```
}
```

a) ResultSet. CONCUR_READ_ONLY

b) ResultSet. CONCUR _INSERTABLE

c) ResultSet. CONCUR _UPDATABLE

d) ResultSet. TYPE_FORWARD_ONLY

e) ResultSet. TYPE_SCROLL_INSENSITIVE

f) ResultSet. TYPE_SCROLL_SENSITIVE

Answer: a, c

147. Which of the following statements is true when the code is run with java AssertDemo?

```
public class AssertDemo {
    public static void main(String [ ] args) {
        Integer x = 10;
        x++ ;
        assert x == null && x>=0;
        System. out. println(x);
        }
 }
```

a) Line 3 generates a compiler error.

b) Line 4 generates a compiler error.

c) Line 5 generates a compiler error.

d) Line 5 throws an AssertionError at runtime.

e) The output is 10.

f) The output is 11.

Answer: f

148. Which of the following are true? (Choose all that apply.)

```
private static void magic(Stream<Integer> s) { Optional o =
s. filter(x -> x < 5). limit(3).max((x, y) -> x-y);
Svstem. out . println(o. get ()); }
```

a) magic (Stream. empty()); runs infinitely.

b) magic (Stream. empty()); throws an exception.

c) magic(stream.iterate(l, x ->x x++)); runs infinitely.

d) magic(stream.iterate(l, x ->>x x++)); throws an exception.

e) magic (Stream. of (5,10)); runs infinitely.

f) magic (Stream. of (5,10)); throws an exception.

g) The method does not compile.

Answer: b, f

149. Suppose that we have the following property files and code. Which bundle is used on lines 7 and 8, respectively?

Dolphins . properties

name=The Dolphin

age=0

Dolphins_fr. properties

name=Dolly

Dolphins _fr _CA. properties

name=Dolly

age=4

Locale fr = new Locale("fr");

ResourceBundle b = ResourceBundle.getBundle("Dolphins", fr);

b. getString("name") ;

b. getString(" age") ;

a) Dolphins . properties and Dolphins. properties

b) Dolphins . properties and Dolphins_fr. properties

c) Dolphins_ fr. properties and Dolphins_fr. properties

d) Dolphins_ fr. properties and Dolphins . properties

e) Dolphins_ fr. properties and Dolphins_fr_CA. properties

f) Dolphins_fr_ CA. properties and Dolphins_fr. properties

Answer: d

150. What is the result of executing the following code? (Choose all that apply.)

```
String line;
Console c = System. console();
if ( (line = c. readLine()) !=null)
    System. out. println(line);
```

a) The code runs without error but prints nothing.

b) The code prints what was entered by the user.

c) An ArraylndexOutOfBoundsException might be thrown.

d) A NullPointerException might be thrown.

e) An IOException might be thrown.

f) The code does not compile.

Answer: b, d

151. What is the result of the following code?

```
public class VisitPark {
    enum AnimalsInPark {
        SQUIRREL, CHIPMUNK, SPARROW;
    }
    public static void main(String[]args) {
        AnimalsInPark[] animals =
AnimalslnPark.values();
    System. out . print In (animals [1] ) ;
  }}
```

a) CHIPMUNK

b) SQUIRREL

c) The code compiles, but the output is indeterminate.

d) A compiler error occurs on line 2.

e) A compiler error occurs on line 6.

f) A compiler error occurs on line 7.

Answer: a

152. Which of the answer choices is printed out by the following code?

```
    String d = Duration. ofDays (1) . toString();
    String p = Period .ofDays(1) .toString();


     boolean bl = d == p;
     boolean b2 = d. equals(p);
System. out.println(bl + "  " +b2);
```

a) false false

b) false true

c) true false

d) true true

e) The code does not compile.

f) A runtime exception is thrown.

Answer: a

153. Assuming that the directory /gorilla exists within the file system with the numerous files including signed-words. txt, what is the result of executing the following code? (Choose all that apply.)

```
Path path = Paths . get ( " / gorilla/ signed-words . txt" ) ;

Files . find (path . getParent() , 10. 0,//k1
       (Path p) -> p.toString() .endsWith(" .txt") && Files.isDirectory(p))
```

```
//k2
      . collect (Collectors. toList())
      . forEach(System. out: : println);

Files. readA11Lines(path) // k3
      .f1atMap(p Stream.of(p. split("
      . map(s -> s.toLowerCase()) // 1<5
      . forEach(System. out: : println);
```

a) The code compiles but does not produce any output at runtime.

b) It does not compile because of line kl.

c) It does not compile because of line k2.

d) It does not compile because of line k3.

e) It does not compile because of line k4.

f) The code prints all of the .txt files in the directory tree.

g) The code prints all of the words in the signed-words .txt file, each on

h) a different line.

Answer: b, c, e

154. Which of the following statements can fill in the blank to make the code compile successfully? (Choose all that apply.)

Set<? extends RuntimeException> set =

______________________________)

a) new HashSet<? extends RuntimeException>();

b) new HashSet<Exception>();

c) new TreeSet<RuntimeException>();

d) new TreeSet<NullPointerException>();

e) None of the above

Answer: c, d

ONLINE RESOURCES

Advanced Java Playlist:

Link : https://www.youtube.com/playlist?list=PLzlh_31VWEFoZXs-3KLPda_DVlN9IPJyg

QR Code :

Java Interview Playlist:

Link: https://www.youtube.com/playlist?list=PLzlh_31VWEFryjvGNIVtyBVYvddpxKexP

QR Code:

Java EE 7 Application Developer (Paper Code - 1Z0-900) Playlist.

Link: https://www.youtube.com/playlist?list=PLzlh_31VWEFodNsy-MeBm7RdKGWAO4TzF

QR Code:

Oracle Certified Professional Java Programmer OCPJP (Paper Code - 1Z0-809) Playlist.

Link: https://www.youtube.com/playlist?list=PLzlh_31VWEFqzXoVrZjKV6cZQKi7iG2D9

QR Code:

Oracle Certified Master Java Enterprise Architect (OCMJEA)(Paper Code - 1Z0-807) Playlist.

Link: https://www.youtube.com/playlist?list=PLzlh_31VWEFqdceCx1Pivwi5ypdvfVaEs

QR Code:

Oracle Certified Master Java Enterprise Architect (OCMJEA)(Paper Code - 1Z0-807) Playlist.

Link: https://www.youtube.com/playlist?list=PLzlh_31VWEFr90bIgv56c3xabjV50iFLV

QR Code:

Core Java Textbook Playlist.

Link: https://www.youtube.com/playlist?list=PLzlh_31VWEFofK7phOZSB9OO9rP1bkaxB

QR Code: